Introduction

Handwriting is an important skill. Acquiring it takes perseverance and practice, whether the writer is left-handed or right-handed. For the left-handed, though, development of the skill of handwriting – in the 'right-handed' world where text runs from left to right – needs just a little more help.

Despite any initial difficulties, with good, regular practice and patient guidance from adults, left-handers can write just as well – and often better – than their right-handed friends. Five to ten minutes of regular daily practice is needed – and this is far more effective than occasional lengthy sessions.

The exercises in this book are intended to be used by the child with adult guidance if necessary. The adult may need to read the instructions to – or with – the child and make sure that the child understands how to form and join the letters correctly. For fluent, neat, legible handwriting to develop, it is important for the child from the start to establish accurate letter formation, smooth and consistent joins and even letter sizing.

The child and adult team should therefore work through the book, practising each skill carefully before moving on to the next. The handwriting style in this book has been chosen to help your child write evenly and fluently. However, the child will eventually develop his or her own unique style.

According to the National Handwriting Association, the series is *"...a structured and attractive course that could help a left-hander become a competent, confident writer."* – and which, according to the Head of School Improvement and Achievement, Worcester LEA, *"...will help to improve the writing skills of all left-handers: a valuable resource for teachers and parents."*

Check this out!

Watch out for the important reminders suggested in the 'Check this out' sections on some of the worksheets.

Basics for successful skill development

Recommended pencil hold and paper position.

Sit Comfortably

Make sure that the child is sitting in a comfortable position and that the desk or table they are using is not too high. Use a cushion on the seat if necessary. Also, ensure the child has plenty of room so that, if they are working with others, they won't clash elbows with a right-handed neighbour.

Positioning the Paper

It is important for the child to turn their paper – or this book – at an angle. This allows the arm to move freely in line with the hand across the page. Turn the top of the page so that the arrow is pointing away from the child and the base of the icon lines up with the edge of the writing table or desk. This will help to develop a consistent working position.

Pencil Hold

It is generally acknowledged that the best way to hold a pencil or pen is in the 'tripod' grip, that is, using three fingers. The pencil rests on the middle finger and is gripped either side by the thumb and forefinger. The pencil should be held about 1.5 cm away from the tip to allow the writing to be seen more clearly. It also keeps the fingers away from the writing. If possible, a straight wrist should be maintained as the child writes along the line, as this will keep the hand below the writing. This is critical when using pen and ink.

Gripping a pencil or pen too tightly is a common problem. It will not improve the handwriting and causes the hand to tire quickly. Use of chunky pencils and pencil grips is helpful (see page 32), as is practice with a marker pen on a whiteboard. Make sure the child turns the board and holds the pen, as above, otherwise the child can lift their hand after writing a line to discover a blank board – all the writing has been rubbed off by their hand.

Word Spacing

Correct spacing between words can be a problem for left-handers. Teachers often tell their pupils to "... leave a finger space between words." The child is encouraged to put their finger (a left hand finger is assumed!) at the end of a word and to begin writing the next word immediately after their finger.

This works well for the right-hander but it leaves left-handers doing contortions! Instead, encourage the left-hander to leave the space required for an imaginary letter 'O' between words.

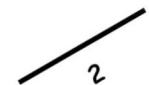

Remember to hold your pencil correctly.

WORKSHEET 1

"Hi, I'm Pencil Pat and I'm going to help you become a really neat writer! So... get your fingers wriggling and try these patterns and letters to warm them up."

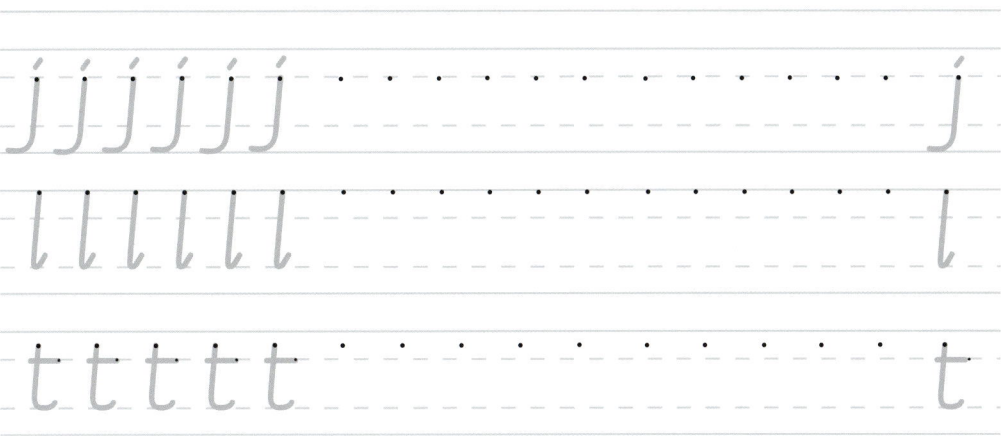

First, trace the pattern above.
Now trace these letters and then complete the row.
Always start at the dots.

i i i i i i i

j j j j j j . . . . j

l l l l l l l

t t t t t . . . . t

u u u u u . . . . u

Trace these letters.

Pencil Pat can...

look up

jump in

turn

Check this out!

1. For a flowing, joined handwriting style, it is easier for left-handers to cross their 't's from right to left.

2. Remember, all these letters start at the top and then the dots or cross are added afterwards.

Now trace this pattern.

Turn your paper clockwise. The base of this arrow icon should line up with the edge of your desk.

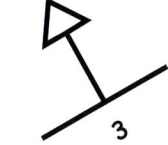

Remember to hold your pencil correctly.

WORKSHEET 2

"Here are some more finger-wriggling patterns to try."

Trace the pattern. Start at the dot and do the whole row without taking your pencil off the paper.

All these letters start at the top and flow from left to right.
Trace these letters and then complete the row.

r r r r r r

n n n n n

m m m m

Check this out!

Try to keep your letters all the same size and make them fit neatly between the lines.

Trace these letters.   Pencil Pat can...

really make a muddle and then make it neat.

Now trace this pattern.

Turn your paper clockwise. The base of this arrow icon should line up with the edge of your desk.

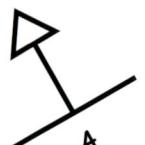

Remember to hold your pencil correctly.

WORKSHEET 3

Pencil Pat and the gang are full of energy today.
Trace this pattern.

· ooooooooooooo

These letters start at the top and flow in a clockwise way.
Trace the letters and then complete the row.

h h h h   h

b b b b   b

k k k k   k

p p p p   p

Check this out!

Are all your letters the same size?

bounce

pop

kick

Trace these bouncing letters.

hop

Now trace this pattern.

ooooooooooo

Turn your paper clockwise. The base of this arrow icon should line up with the edge of your desk.

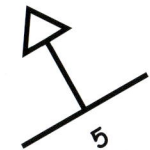

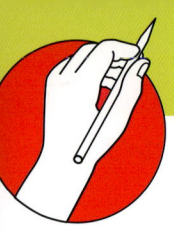

Remember to hold your pencil correctly.

WORKSHEET 4

Trace the patterns and letters
as Pencil Pat gets ready to jump!

· ○○○○○○○○○○○○

All these letters flow in an anticlockwise direction.
Trace the letters and then complete the row.

c c c c c   c

o o o o o   o

e e e e e   e

Trace these letters.

Pencil Pat...

easily   jump

can

over

Now trace this pattern.

· ○○○○○○○○○○○○

Turn your paper clockwise. The base of this arrow icon should line up with the edge of your desk.

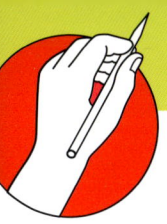

Remember to hold your pencil correctly.

WORKSHEET 5

"Pencil Pat and the gang like to draw. Do you?"

Trace this pattern.

All these letters flow in an anticlockwise direction.
Trace the letters and then complete the row.

a a a a a   a

d d d d d   d

g g g g g   g

Pencil Pat and his buddies can...

doodle away

great

Trace these letters.

Now trace this pattern.

Turn your paper clockwise. The base of this arrow icon should line up with the edge of your desk.

Remember to hold your pencil correctly.

WORKSHEET 6

"It's a challenge! Can you draw a square fish? What would you call it?"

Trace this pattern.

All these letters begin in an anticlockwise direction.
Trace the letters and then complete the row.

Pencil Pat and his chums can...

draw a square fish

Trace these letters.

Now trace this pattern.

Turn your paper clockwise. The base of this arrow icon should line up with the edge of your desk.

Remember to hold your pencil correctly.

WORKSHEET 7

Pencil Pat and the gang are keeping fit!
Exercise your fingers first by tracing these patterns!

All these letters have a zigzag shape. Trace and complete.

v v v v v　　　　　　　　　　v

w w w w　　　　　　　　　　w

Pencil Pat and the team can...
walk
everywhere

Trace the letters.

Trace and complete.

x x x x x　　　　　　　　　　x

y y y y y　　　　　　　　　　y

z z z z z　　　　　　　　　　z

Now trace these letters.   Pencil Pat can...
play the xylophone
with zest.

Turn your paper clockwise. The base of this arrow icon should line up with the edge of your desk.

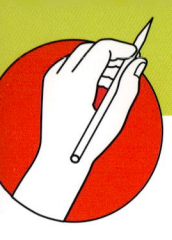

Remember to hold your pencil correctly.

WORKSHEET 8

Are you ready for some funky stuff? Pencil Pat says:
"It's time to begin joining up your letters."

First, trace this pattern.

Trace these letters and then complete the row.

ai

ai ai

ar

ar ar

Check this out!

Don't press down too hard —
you might make a hole in the paper!

un

un un

Now trace this pattern.

Turn your paper clockwise. The base of this arrow icon should line up with the edge of your desk.

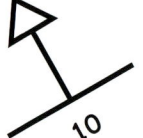

 Remember to hold your pencil correctly.

WORKSHEET 9

"Don't get your fingers in a twist," says Pencil Pat.

Trace and copy these words.

air lair hair pair

air lair hair pair

Now trace this pattern.

Check this out!

Remember to cross the 't's from right to left!

Trace and copy these words.

bar car tar ear

bar car tar ear

Now trace this pattern.

"If you've got this far, you're doing really well!"

Turn your paper clockwise. The base of this arrow icon should line up with the edge of your desk.

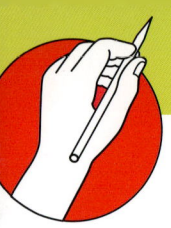

Remember to hold your pencil correctly.

WORKSHEET 10

Pencil Pat's pal is learning to play the guitar.

Do you know this song: 'Row, row, row your boat, gently down the stream.'? Try singing it slowly as you trace the patterns on this page!

A rythmn can help you get a nice writing flow.

Trace and copy these words.

bun   nun   sun   sung

bun   nun   sun   sung

Trace this pattern.

Trace and copy these words.

bump   hump   lump

bump   hump   lump

Now trace this pattern.

Turn your paper clockwise. The base of this arrow icon should line up with the edge of your desk.

WORKSHEET 11

"Get ready to make these letters join," says Pencil Pat.

First, trace the pattern.

Now trace and copy these letters.

ou

ou ou

vi

vi vi

wi

wi wi

Check this out!

Don't hold your pen or pencil too tightly — it doesn't make your writing any better and your fingers will get tired.

Now trace this pattern.

Turn your paper clockwise. The base of this arrow icon should line up with the edge of your desk.

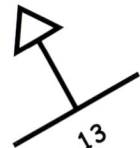

Remember to hold your pencil correctly.

WORKSHEET 12

Pencil Pat and his crew are fishing.

Trace and copy these words.

or   rod   row   vow

or   rod   row   vow

"Have a go at these exercises — but don't rock the boat!"

First, trace this pattern.

Check this out!

Try to keep your letters all the same size and make them fit neatly between the lines.

Now trace and copy these letter patterns.

acacacacacacacacacaca

unununununununununun

Turn your paper clockwise. The base of this arrow icon should line up with the edge of your desk.

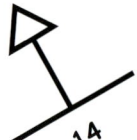

Remember to hold your pencil correctly.

WORKSHEET 13

Hop your fingers along with Pencil Pat as you trace and copy these words.

First, trace this pattern.

Trace and copy these words.

big   pig   dog   log

bow   cow   sun   bun

pin   tin   hop   mop

Pencil Pat likes playing with words.

Now trace this pattern.

Turn your paper clockwise. The base of this arrow icon should line up with the edge of your desk.

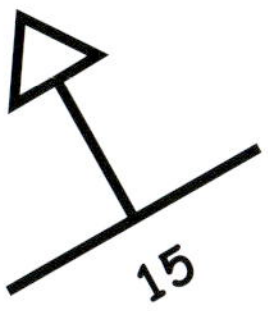

15

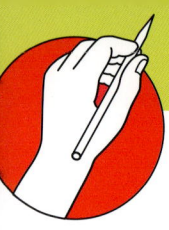

WORKSHEET 14

Pencil Pat and the gang are busily drawing patterns.
You can practise the patterns in this book.
Use the lined paper on page 31.

Trace this pattern.

Trace and copy these letters.

ab

ab ab

ut

ut ut

it

it it

Check this out!

For a flowing joined handwriting style, it is easier for left-handers to cross their 't's from right to left.

Now trace this pattern.

"Gosh!" Pencil Pat says. "You are halfway through this book now — and you're doing very well. Keep it up!"

Turn your paper clockwise. The base of this arrow icon should line up with the edge of your desk.

Remember to hold your pencil correctly.

16

 Remember to hold your pencil correctly.

WORKSHEET 15

"These patterns should make your fingers dizzy," says Pencil Pat!

Trace and copy these words with Pencil Pat and his posse.

dab nab pull bull

dab nab pull bull

"Be careful! That bull looks angry, Pencil Pat!"

bit hit lit sit

bit hit lit sit

Check this out!

Remember to cross the 't's and dot the 'i's at the end of each word.

Now trace this pattern.

Turn your paper clockwise. The base of this arrow icon should line up with the edge of your desk.

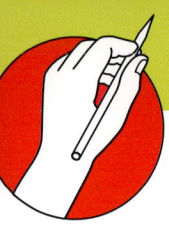

Remember to hold your pencil correctly.

WORKSHEET 16

Pencil Pat and the gang all have different hobbies.
Guess which clubs they belong to.

Trace this pattern.

Check this out!

Try to keep your letters all the same size and make them fit between the lines.

Now trace and copy these words.

hat   bat   cut   nut

hat   bat   cut   nut

Trace and copy these letter patterns.

lblblblblblblblblblbl

hlhlhlhlhlhlhlhlhlhl

Turn your paper clockwise. The base of this arrow icon should line up with the edge of your desk.

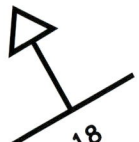

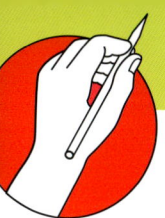

Remember to hold your pencil correctly.

WORKSHEET 17

Pencil Pat's friends are enjoying practising their writing!

Trace this pattern.

Now join these letters up with Pencil Pat's buddies.
Trace and copy the letters.

Now trace these patterns.

Check this out!

Remember not to press down too hard or hold your pencil too tightly.

Turn your paper clockwise. The base of this arrow icon should line up with the edge of your desk.

Remember to hold your pencil correctly.

WORKSHEET 18

Pencil Pat and the group are having fun!

Trace and copy these words with Pencil Pat's friends.
As you trace the patterns, say the words "old, cold, hot, pot, old, cold, hot, pot." in time with your writing.

Check this out!

Remember to cross the 't's from right to left!

old cold hot pot

old cold hot pot

Now trace these patterns.

Trace and copy these words.

wham   whack

wham   whack

Turn your paper clockwise. The base of this arrow icon should line up with the edge of your desk.

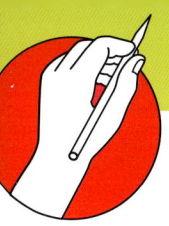

Remember to hold your pencil correctly.

WORKSHEET 19

It's quiz time. Pencil Pat and the gang are making their brains work hard today!

Trace and copy these question words with Pencil Pat's puzzled pals.

why?   who?   what?

why?   who?   what?

Check this out!

Are all your letters the same size and do they fit neatly between the lines?

Now trace this mad pattern.

Trace and copy these letter patterns.

whwhwhwhwhwhwh

olololololololololololol

Turn your paper clockwise. The base of this arrow icon should line up with the edge of your desk.

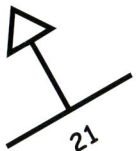

WORKSHEET 20

Remember to hold your pencil correctly.

"Look before you leap, Pencil Pat.
Then maybe you won't end up in a puddle!"

Trace and then copy this letter pattern.

e

eeeeeeeeeeeeeeeeeee

Trace and copy these words.

leg   leap   heap

leg   leap   heap

Now trace this pattern.

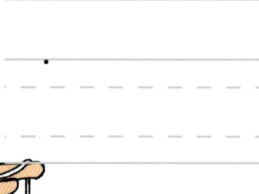

Trace and copy.

web   well   wet

web   well   wet

Turn your paper clockwise. The base of this arrow icon should line up with the edge of your desk.

Remember to hold your pencil correctly.

WORKSHEET 21

Pencil Pat's troupe are putting on a circus show!

Trace and copy these letters.

rr   rt

rrtrrtrrtrrtrrtrrtrrt

Trace and copy these words.

circus   ring

hurtle

Check this out!

Remember to cross the 't's from right to left!

turtle

Where did Pat find that turtle?

Now trace this pattern.

Turn your paper clockwise. The base of this arrow icon should line up with the edge of your desk.

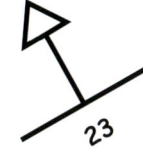

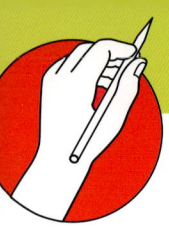

Remember to hold your pencil correctly.

WORKSHEET 22

"Pencil Pat and the others are treasure-hunting. What have they found?"

Trace and copy these letter patterns.

re

rererererererererere

Trace and copy these words.

treasure   *trove*

seashore   *shell*

Pencil Pat has a map and is ready to dig for treasure.

Now trace this pattern.

Turn your paper clockwise. The base of this arrow icon should line up with the edge of your desk.

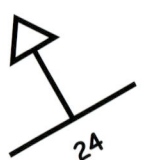

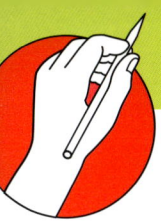

Remember to hold your pencil correctly.

WORKSHEET 23

Pencil Pat says:
"Look carefully — some of these letters don't join!"

Trace and copy these letters.

jo   yo   go

jygjygjygjygjygjygjyg

Trace and copy these words.

jogging   jaguar

yellow   jelly

Pencil Pat says: "Never try to run with a jelly!"

Turn your paper clockwise. The base of this arrow icon should line up with the edge of your desk.

Remember to hold your pencil correctly.

WORKSHEET 24

Today, Pencil Pat has gone to the beach with his mates.

Trace and complete these letters.

ff

Cross the 'ff's at the end of each pair.

ff ff ff ff ff ff ff ff ff ff

Now write your own 'ff's.

Trace and copy these words.

puffer   *fish*   *surf*

Check this out!

Look carefully — some of the letters don't join.

Pencil Pat is a bit squeamish about squid.

Trace and copy these words.

Turn your paper clockwise. The base of this arrow icon should line up with the edge of your desk.

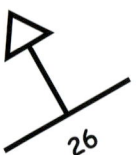

 Remember to hold your pencil correctly.

WORKSHEET 25

"Look out! Here are some more tricky letter joins."

Trace and copy these letter patterns and words.

ozo   oxi

zzzzzzzzzzzz

Check this out!

Look carefully — some of the letters don't join.

For extra practice, use the Practice Sheet on page 31.

Trace and copy these words.

zany   zebras

Pencil Pat — don't tear that zebra suit!

boxing   foxes

Now trace this pattern.

ooooooooooo

"Well done — you have finished all the joins!"

Turn your paper clockwise. The base of this arrow icon should line up with the edge of your desk.

Remember to hold your pencil correctly.

WORKSHEET 26

IT'S PARTY TIME! All of Pencil Pat's friends are here to join the gang for a party.

Write these CAPITAL letters.
Check out CAPITAL letter formation on page 33.
Trace and copy each friend's name.

F E L

Fred Emma Liam

I T A

Ivor Tara Ali

M N V

Mark Nick Val

Pencil Pat has lots more friends for you to meet...

Turn your paper clockwise. The base of this arrow icon should line up with the edge of your desk.

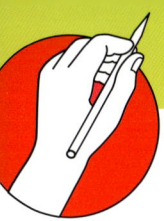

Remember to hold your pencil correctly.

WORKSHEET 27

"Here are some more of my mates.
Yes, even the dog has come to my party!"

Write these CAPITAL letters.
Trace and copy each friend's name.

W	H	K
Wilf	Holly	Kyle

X	Y	Z
Xenia	Yasmin	Zack

B	D	P
Ben	Daisy	Paul

"Who else is coming to the party?"

Turn your paper clockwise. The base of this arrow icon should line up with the edge of your desk.

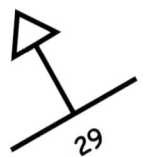

Remember to hold your pencil correctly.

WORKSHEET 28

Here are the rest of Pencil Pat's friends ready to join the fun!

Write these CAPITAL letters.
Trace and copy each friend's name.

R   C   G

Rob   Chloe   Gus

O   Q   S

Omar   Queeny   Sam

J   U

Josh   Una

"Hurray! Well done!
You've made it to the end of this book."

Turn your paper clockwise. The base of this arrow icon should line up with the edge of your desk.

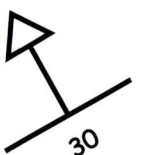

Remember to hold your pencil correctly.

PRACTICE SHEET

Check this out!

You can photocopy this page and use it for more practice.

Turn your paper clockwise. The base of this arrow icon should line up with the edge of your desk.

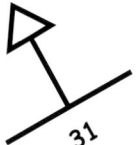

REFERENCE SHEET

Check this out!

Use this page as a handy reference for independent writing.

a b c d e
f g h i j k
l m n o p
q r s t u
v w x y z

REFERENCE SHEET

Check this out!

Use this page as a handy reference for independent writing.

33

More help for left-handers

Many products have been designed for use with the left hand. There are also specialist centres which offer advice for left-handers, their parents and teachers, and which supply products for left-handed use. Some of the items which relate to activities in this book are described below, but there are many other invaluable everyday devices available for both children and adults. These range from sloping desks to can openers, scissors to secateurs and even golf clubs and electric guitars. A few of the centres around the world which supply products for left-handers, or offer educational advice on left-handed issues, are listed below.

A DVD entitled *Left-Handed Children – A Guide for Teachers and Parents*, by the authors of this series and endorsed by the Teacher Training Agency, is available via the authors' own website – *leftshoponline.co.uk* – which also carries details of the teacher training workshops provided by Mark Stewart.

Educational Products

Pencils, Pens and Sharpeners

Faber Castell's Jumbo triangular pencils, with raised resin dots for extra purchase for the fingers, are excellent. Available separately or in packs of 6 or 12 crayons, Jumbos are a good size for young children. There is also a thinner version called Grip 2001 which has raised resin dots.

Stabilo produces an excellent pen called the EASYoriginal Graffiti. Make sure you get the 'Graffiti' version! It has the grip moulded into the barrel, like the EASYergo pencil by the same company. This pen helps to maintain the same dynamic tripod grip throughout your child's school life.

With the EASYoriginal Graffiti, each time a new cartridge is inserted a new nib is automatically introduced. The ink can also be erased.

Schneider has also produced a very useful pen. It has a rollerball nib but uses ordinary ink cartridges. It also has a tripod grip. This is a great pen for school use.

There are also left-handed pencil sharpeners. These are held in the right hand, and the pencil is turned away from the body. Usually with two holes, the larger hole offers reasonable sharpening for triangular pencils.

Scissors

These can be either right- or left-handed, *not* both. Proper left-handed scissors have the blades set so that, when held either way up in the left hand, the cutting edge is clearly visible on the inside of the scissors. Not being able to use scissors, particularly at a young age, can cause frustration and loss of self-esteem.

Further Reading

The Left-hander's Handbook by Diane G Paul
Published by Robinswood Press.
ISBN 978-1869981-594

So You Think They're Left-Handed?
by Mark and Heather Stewart
Published by Robinswood Press.
ISBN 978-1906053-956